From Your Friends At **The M**

SEPTEMBER

A MONTH OF REPRODUCIBLES AT YOUR FINGERTIPS!

Grade 1

Editor:
Susan Hohbach Walker

Writers:
Catherine Broome, Lisa Buchholz, Amy Erickson,
Amy Harders, Lucia Kemp Henry,
Cynthia Holcomb, Sharon Murphy

Art Coordinator:
Clevell Harris

Artists:
Cathy Spangler Bruce, Teresa Davidson,
Nick Greenwood, Clevell Harris, Rob Mayworth,
Kimberly Richard, Donna K. Teal

Cover Artist:
Jennifer Tipton Bennett

www.themailbox.com

©1998 by THE EDUCATION CENTER, INC.
All rights reserved.
ISBN10 #1-56234-260-6 • ISBN13 #978-156234-260-9

Manufactured in the United States
10 9 8 7

Table Of Contents

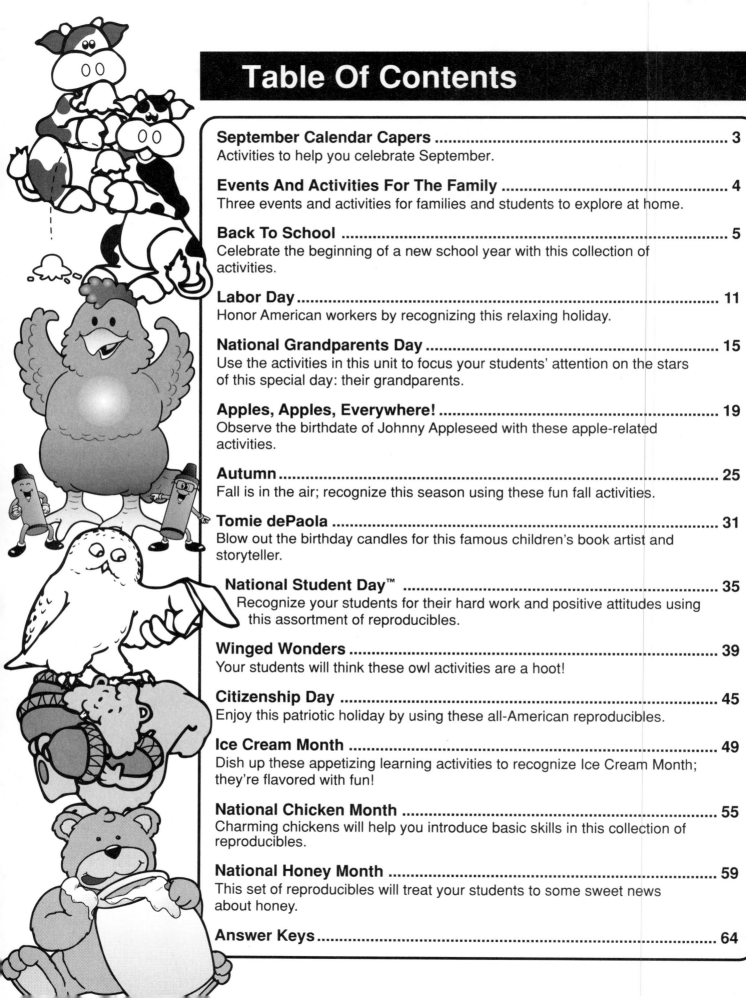

September Calendar Capers

Monday	Tuesday	Wednesday	Thursday	Friday
Labor Day (the first Monday in September) honors working people. Have students list workers who helped them last week.	September is Library Card Sign-Up Month. Encourage each student to visit the public library with his parents and sign up for his own library card. RICHMOND COUNTY PUBLIC LIBRARY 9/1/98 Josh Teal	The first Kodak® camera was patented on September 4, 1888. Honor the inventor, George Eastman, by taking snapshots of your students and displaying them in your classroom.	September is Children's Eye Health And Safety Month. Read aloud *Arthur's Eyes* by Marc Brown (Little, Brown And Company; 1986) and discuss with students the importance of eye care.	What are your students' hopes for this year? Have each youngster draw a picture of what she'd like to learn or do during this school year.
September is Ice Cream Month. Take a class survey of favorite ice-cream flavors; then graph the results with students.	Have each student list the letters of *September* in a column. Then challenge him to write a fun fall activity that begins with each letter. Soccer games Eating pumpkin pie Playing with friends T E M B E R	September 8 is National Pledge Of Allegiance Day. Recite the pledge with students; then discuss what a *pledge* is and the meaning of this one.	September 10 is Swap Ideas Day. Encourage students to share their thoughts and creativity by having them swap ideas with one another.	September 12 is the birthdate of Jesse Owens, a four-time gold medal winner in the 1936 Olympic® Games. Have each student draw a picture of a runner crossing a finish line. GOLD
The Pilgrims left England on the *Mayflower* on September 16, 1620. Read aloud *If You Sailed On The Mayflower* by Ann McGovern (Scholastic Inc., 1991).	Citizenship Day is celebrated on September 17. Discuss with students the rights and responsibilities of an American citizen.	Brainstorm autumn words with students. Then have each youngster select a specified number of words and write them in ABC order. apple pumpkin leaf	The last full week in September is National Dog Care Week. Discuss proper dog care with students. Then have each youngster make a poster by writing and illustrating a dog-care tip on a large sheet of paper.	The first ice-cream cone was made of paper, and a patent for it was filed on September 22, 1903. Celebrate the birth of the cone by having an ice-cream party.
Remind students that fall begins on or near September 22. Have each student cut out fall pictures from discarded magazines and glue them onto paper to make an autumn collage.	Celebrate the birthdate of Jim Henson, creator of the Muppets® characters, on September 24 by reading aloud a book featuring a Muppet® character. Then have each student create a sock puppet.	Recognize Johnny Appleseed's birth anniversary on September 26 with a tasty apple snack, such as apple and cheese wedges or homemade applesauce.	Have each student write a poem about the colors of fall. Instruct her to begin with this phrase: "Fall is red like..." and to use this sentence pattern throughout her poem. Fall is red like apples. Fall is brown like leaves.	Ask each student to draw a picture of a highlight from this month. FIRST PLACE

©1998 The Education Center, Inc. • *September Monthly Reproducibles* • Grade 1 • TEC956

Note To The Teacher: Highlight special days and events with these fact-filled ideas.

September
Events And Activities For The Family

Directions: Select at least one activity below to complete as a family by the end of September. *(Challenge: See if your family can complete all three activities.)*

Children's Eye Health And Safety Month

Develop an eye for clues with this family guessing activity! Choose a characteristic from the list below; then put on a pair of sunglasses or hold a pair of construction-paper glasses to your eyes. Without revealing it, identify an item in the room that has the chosen characteristic. Then state, "I spy something that [characteristic]." Challenge your family members to guess the described item. After someone correctly identifies it, have him or her use the eyeglasses to spy the next item and give a related clue. Continue in a like manner, until each of you has taken several turns giving clues. Now that's out-of-sight learning fun!

Characteristics
- Begins with [letter]
- Ends with [consonant]
- Rhymes with [word family]
- Has [number] syllables

Happy Birthday, Bernard Waber!

Author and illustrator Bernard Waber is the creator of the beloved Lyle The Crocodile and Ira characters. Celebrate his birthday on September 27 by reading to your child one of his many delightful books, such as *Lyle At The Office* (Houghton Mifflin Company, 1996) or *Gina* (Houghton Mifflin Company, 1997). Explain that Waber first became involved with children's books as an illustrator. But it wasn't long before he began writing *and* illustrating his own original children's stories. Have your child use Waber's whimsical artwork as a model to paint a picture on a large sheet of paper. Then ask your youngster to write a story about it. What a great way to promote reading and writing!

Dear Diary Day

Try this memorable idea "write" away! In recognition of Dear Diary Day on September 22, help your child begin a diary. To make a diary, staple several blank sheets of paper between construction-paper covers and have your child personalize the covers as desired. Each day after school, ask your child to write and draw about his or her day in the diary. Be sure to help your child date each entry. No doubt this diary will be a cherished keepsake. And it will provide a meaningful way for your child to practice writing!

Note To The Teacher: Distribute one copy of this reproducible to each student at the beginning of the month. Encourage each family to complete at least one activity by the end of September.

Back To School

The start of a new school year is an exciting time for students, parents, and teachers. It marks the end of the summer and the beginning of a fun-filled, challenging year. So start back to school in style with these motivating activities.

First-Day Fun

Your students will be thrilled to take home a booklet from their first day of school. Each child will have a sense of accomplishment as he completes the pages of this first-day memento. Use the following directions to guide students in completing this clever keepsake.

Directions:

1. Give each child one copy of each of the following pages: 8, 9, and 10.
2. Instruct each student to cut apart the six booklet pages along the heavy, solid lines.
3. Assist each student in entering the information on the booklet cover. Ask him to write his name where indicated.
4. Guide each child in completing the following activities:

   Booklet page 1: Draw a self-portrait next to the desk.

   Booklet page 2: Circle and color the method he used to get to school.

   Booklet page 3: Draw the items he brought with him to school.

   Booklet page 4: Color the appropriate crayon with the matching color.

   Booklet page 5: Write the teacher's name, and draw a picture of his teacher.

5. Have each child sequence his pages behind the cover. Staple along the left margin.

Classy Communication

Getting the new school year off to a great start means establishing a line of parent communication. Use the decorative stationery on page 6 to inform parents about items such as introductory information, classroom news, classroom rules and expectations, daily schedules, and special events.

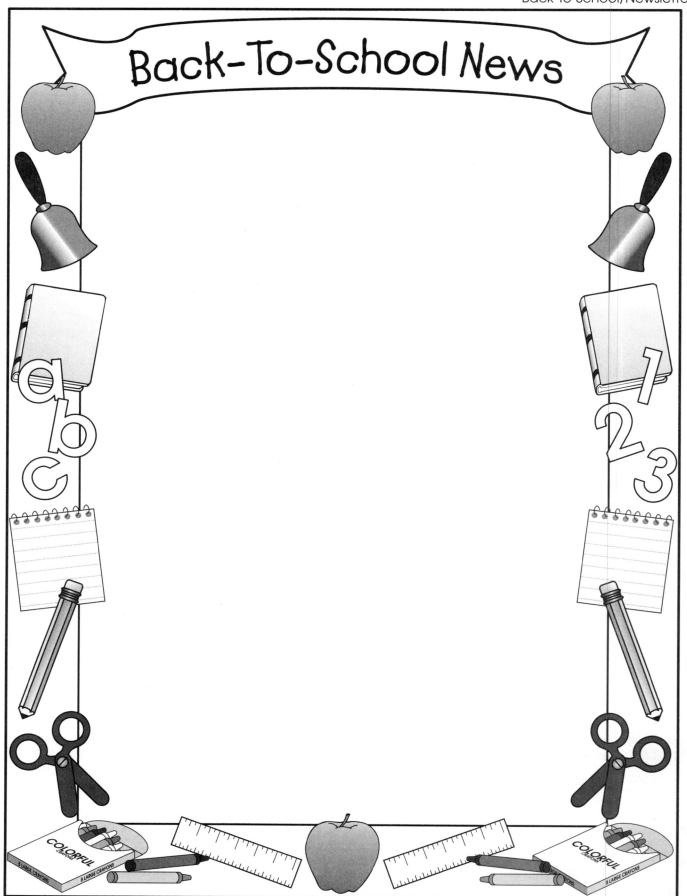

Back-To-School News

Note To The Teacher: Use with "Classy Communication" on page 5.

Name_____

Tool Time

 Cut.

Glue to finish each pattern.

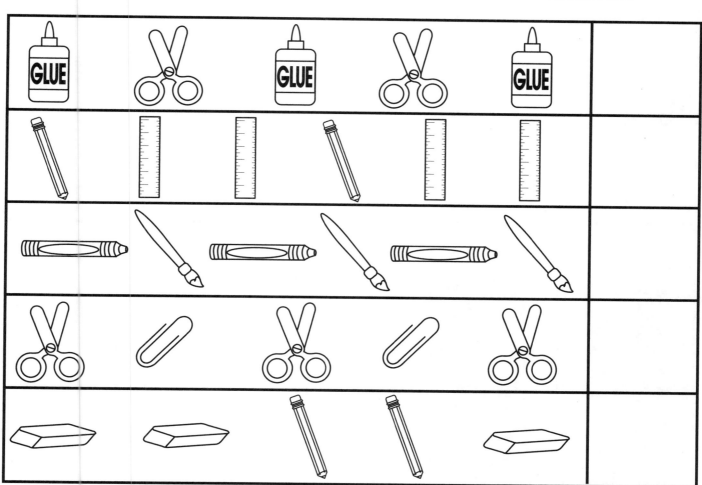

©1998 The Education Center, Inc. • *September Monthly Reproducibles* • Grade 1 • TEC956

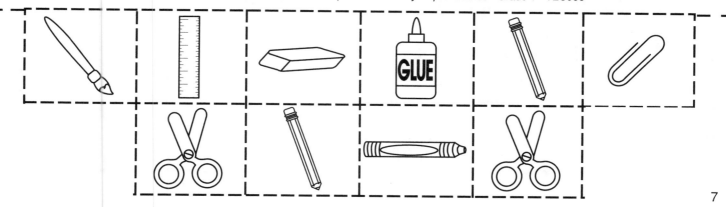

This is me on my first day of school.

School is fun! ☺

I am in the first grade.

1

Read All About My First Day!

WELCOME!

Grade 1

Room: _____

Teacher: _____

Name _____

©1998 The Education Center, Inc. • September Monthly Reproducibles • Grade 1 • TEC956

Note To The Teacher: Use pages 8, 9, and 10 with "First-Day Fun" on page 5.

This is what I brought in my backpack.

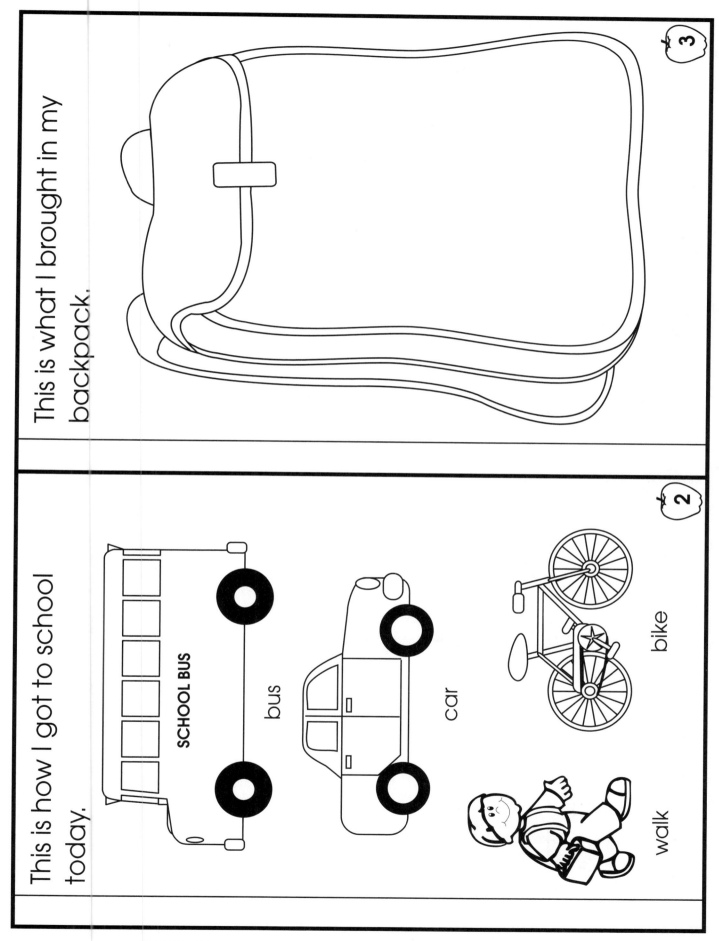

3

This is how I got to school today.

SCHOOL BUS

bus

car

bike

walk

2

My teacher's name is

_____

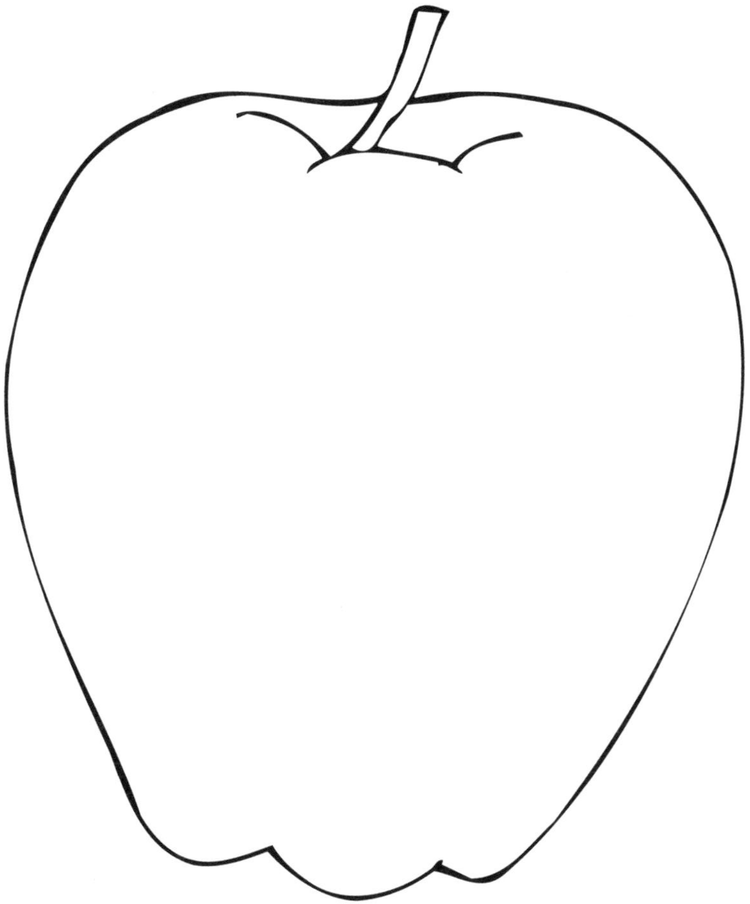

It's going to be a good year!

My favorite color is

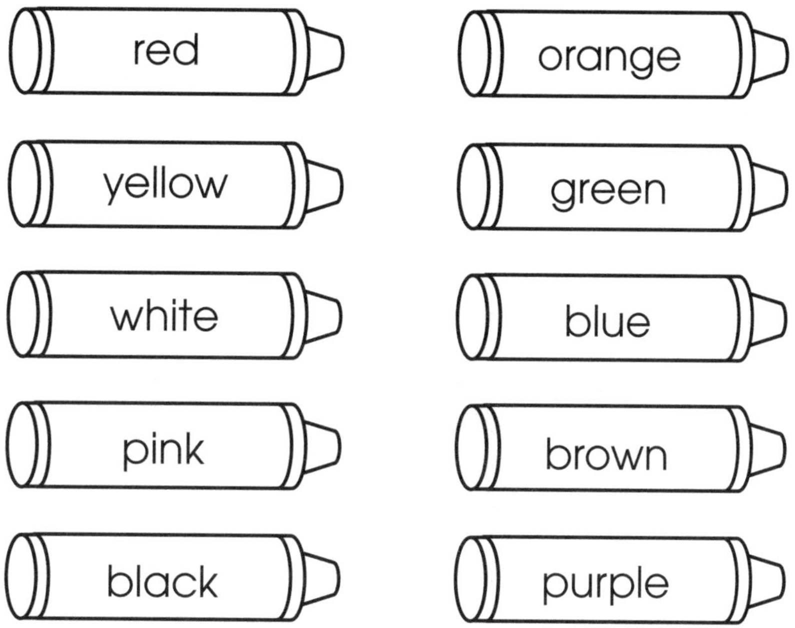

orange
green
blue
brown
purple

red
yellow
white
pink
black

COLORFUL
CRAYONS
8 LARGE CRAYONS
8 LARGE CRAYONS

LABOR DAY

What better way to honor American workers than to give them a day off work! And that's just what happens on Labor Day. This celebration was first held in New York City on September 5, 1882. It was proclaimed a federal holiday in 1894 and is celebrated annually on the first Monday of September. There are often parades, speakers, and picnics held in honor of our country's workers.

The Business Of Learning

These creative activities will familiarize your students with local workers and businesses while reinforcing several important skills. Challenge your students to collect business cards from friends, relatives, and local business-people. Combine students' collections into a large class resource; then try one or more of the following activities with your students:

— Have students sort the cards using a variety of categories, such as type of business (plumbers, hairstylists, real estate agents, etc.), zip code, area code, or color.
— Have students alphabetize a portion of the cards using the names of the businesses.
— Encourage students to read several cards carefully, looking for a key sight word such as *the* or *at.*
— Challenge students to read the cards looking for predetermined punctuation marks (apostrophes, quotation marks, etc.).
— Display the cards on a bulletin board and ask students to tell how they think the person named on each card would do his or her job.

For a fun follow-up, help each child make a set of personal "business" cards. This can either be done by using a computer or by cutting construction paper into 2" x 3" pieces and writing the information on the cards.

Labor Day Lotto

Use this fun lotto variation to review a variety of jobs with your students. Distribute a copy of page 14, along with some game markers, to each child. Ask her to cut out the picture squares on the bottom of the page. Instruct her to randomly program each of the 16 squares by gluing a cutout atop each blank square. While students are programming their gameboards, cut a set of picture squares from an additional copy of page 14 and place them in a container. To play the game, draw a square from the container and read it aloud. Each student locates the announced worker on her board, then covers it. The first student to cover four squares in a row shouts out, "Happy Labor Day!" To win the game, she must read aloud the jobs from the four squares she covered. If desired, award the winning student with a sticker or another small prize.

Name_____

Head Count

Count the dots.

Write the number.

painter	nurse	police officer	chef
_ _ _ _ _	_ _ _ _ _	_ _ _ _ _	_ _ _ _ _
_____	_____	_____	_____

engineer	construction worker	astronaut	firefighter
_ _ _ _ _	_ _ _ _ _	_ _ _ _ _	_ _ _ _ _
_____	_____	_____	_____

farmer	reporter	sailor	artist
_ _ _ _ _	_ _ _ _ _	_ _ _ _ _	_ _ _ _ _
_____	_____	_____	_____

Which hat would you like to wear? _____

✏ Write.   **Future Plans**

When I grow up, I want to be

_____

- -

_____

I would like this job because

_____

- -

_____

- -

_____

- -

I will need to learn

_____

- -

_____

- -

I will wear

_____

- -

_____

Name_____

Labor Day Lotto

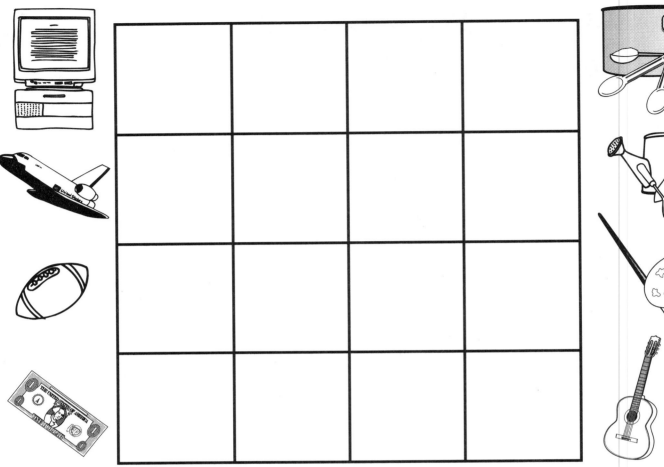

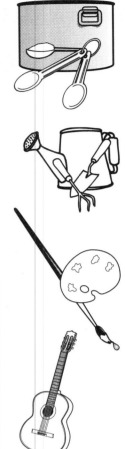

©1998 The Education Center, Inc. • *September Monthly Reproducibles* • Grade 1 • TEC968

mechanic · hairstylist · painter · astronaut · baker · florist

musician · dentist · teacher · firefighter · police officer

pilot · athlete · farmer · banker · doctor

14   **Note To The Teacher:** Use with "Labor Day Lotto" on page 11.

NATIONAL GRANDPARENTS DAY

The relationship between a child and his or her grandparents is a very special one. Honor that bond by celebrating National Grandparents Day on the first Sunday after Labor Day.

Grandparent Greetings

These Grandparents Day cards are full of personality. Distribute a copy of page 18 to each child and ask him to cut out the person pattern and the letter form along the heavy solid outlines. Explain the letter format and assist each student in writing a letter to a grandparent or another special adult. Next provide an assortment of craft items such as yarn, fabric scraps, buttons, sequins, dry pasta, etc. Have each child use the items to create a likeness of his grandparent by gluing the items onto the person pattern. Finally, provide each child with a 9" x 12" sheet of construction paper. After folding the paper to form a card, have each child glue his completed letter to the inside and the person pattern to the front of the card. Grandparents will be delighted with this adorable keepsake!

Grandparent Name Game

Do your students have a Granny? A Pop Pop? Or a Nanna? Play this exciting game with your class to enlighten them about the variety of endearing names we give to our grandparents. In advance, have each student think about special names he calls his grandparents. (Encourage children without grandparents to think of other older adults who are special to them.) Get the game started by having all students stand in a circle. Then recite the poem below, inserting the nickname of *your* grandmother and a student's name where indicated. Then let the game take off by having the named child repeat the rhyme inserting *his* grandmother's nickname and the name of another student. After the named child says the rhyme, have him be seated on the floor. Continue with each named child until all students have had a chance to share. Then repeat the rhyme using the word *grandpa* in place of *grandma* and *his* instead of *her* in the second line. Expect lots of giggles and smiles from your class during this activity!

> I call my grandma [grandmother's nickname];
> That's her special name.
> I want to know what [student's name] says
> To hear if it's the same.

Grandma And Grandpa In The Kitchen

Here's a fun way to review map skills during your National Grandparents Day celebration. Give each child a copy of page 17. Instruct her to cut the grandmother and grandfather manipulatives along the dotted lines. Then have her fold where indicated to make stand-up figures. Discuss the objects on the map's key; then lead your class in answering the following questions and completing the listed activities.

- How many plants are in Grandma and Grandpa Clutter's kitchen?
- Is the stove next to the sink or next to the refrigerator?
- How many tables are in the kitchen?
- Grandma Clutter needs to wash some dishes. Show her standing by the sink.
- Grandpa Clutter needs some milk to make a cake. Show him standing near the refrigerator.
- Where would Grandma and Grandpa sit to eat dinner? Put them each on a chair.

Kitchen Clutter!

Grandma and Grandpa need help cleaning up the kitchen.

Draw an **x** if it does not belong.

Cut.

Glue to match each set.

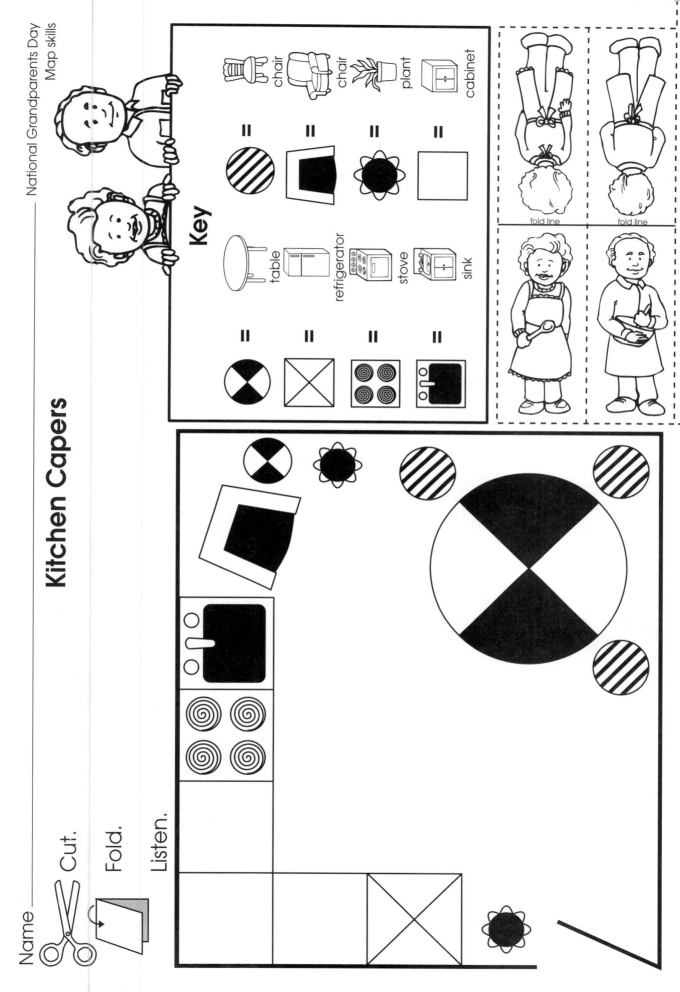

Name

Kitchen Capers

Cut.

Fold.

Listen.

Key

chair = (striped circle)

chair = (black square)

plant = (flower circle)

cabinet = (square)

table = (black circle with X)

refrigerator = (square with X)

stove = (four burners)

sink = (sink)

fold line   fold line

©1998 The Education Center, Inc. • *September Monthly Reproducibles* • Grade 1 • TEC956

Note To The Teacher: Use with "Grandma And Grandpa In The Kitchen" on page 15.

Grandparent Greetings

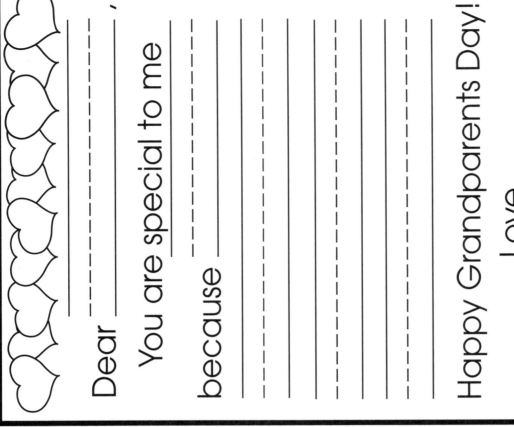

Dear _____,

You are special to me _____

because _____

_____

_____

_____

Happy Grandparents Day!

Love,

_____

Note To The Teacher: Use with "Grandparent Greetings" on page 15.

Apples, Apples, Everywhere!

Celebrate the abundant apple season by observing Johnny Appleseed's birthday on September 26. Johnny Appleseed, born John Chapman, spent over half of his life in the Ohio River valley, planting seeds and giving away tree saplings to begin the building of apple orchards throughout the Midwest. Use the activities and reproducibles in this unit to take a big bite of the delicious legacy that Johnny gave to all of us.

All Kinds Of Apples

Although Johnny was probably an expert on many varieties of apples, your youngsters may actually be familiar with only a few. Bring lots of different apples in all colors into the classroom, including Delicious, Golden Delicious, Gala, Granny Smith, Jonathan, McIntosh, and Winesap. Have your students help you sort and classify this mass of apples into smaller sets by color; then invite your youngsters to take part in a taste test. After each child has sampled a slice of each type of apple, ask the class to vote and award titles to the Reddest Apple, the Sweetest Apple, the Tastiest Apple, the Most Tart Apple, and the Best Apple Of The Bunch!

Artful Apples

Encourage each child to take her pick of any apple (see "All Kinds Of Apples" on this page) to interpret in this brightly colored collage project. Have each child study her green, red, or yellow apple for the lovely variations in the color of its skin; then challenge her to reproduce the colors she sees using the following technique. Provide each child with an apple-shaped, poster-board cutout (about 9" x 9"). Then give her a choice of several tissue-paper pieces in some of the following colors: pink, red, orange, yellow, light green, dark green, gold, and light brown. Also provide each student with a paintbrush and a container of white glue thinned with water. Ask each student to brush a small area of the cutout with the glue mixture and lay torn pieces of colored tissue atop the glue. Then have her brush more glue over the tissue-covered area. Encourage students to mix and blend different colors of tissue as they completely cover their apple shapes.

Apple Alphabet

Fill in Johnny Appleseed's alphabet.

✏️ Write.

Bonus Box: Color the consonants **red.**
Color the vowels **green.**

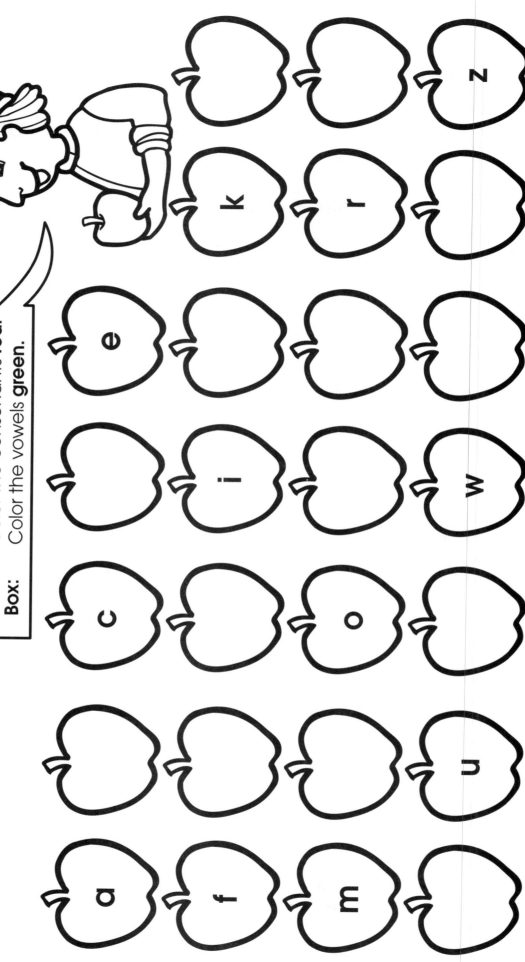

Name_____

Matching Apples

Find the pictures that rhyme.

Cut.

Glue.

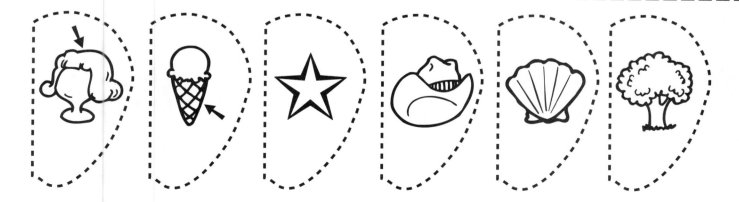

Name_____

Johnny's Opposites

Look at each picture.

Find the opposite.

 Cut.

 Glue.

 little		cold		 hard	
night		 happy		 down	

 sad  hot  up  soft  big  day

22

Name_____

Jolly Johnny

Color by the code.

Color Code
b = red
f = blue
m = green
s = yellow
t = orange

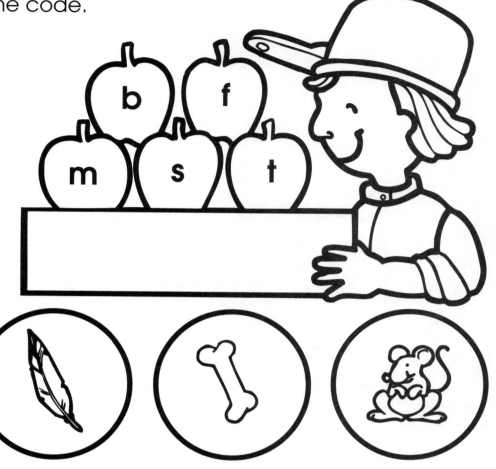

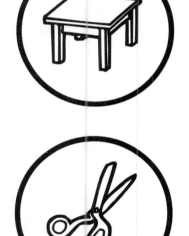

Name_____

Count The Crop

 Count each set.

 Write the number.

 Cut out the number words.

Glue.

one   three   four   five   six   seven   eight   nine   ten

AUTUMN

Change is in the air! Jump into autumn with this bumper crop of fall fun. Your students will be absolutely nuts about it!

Fall Facts

- The first day of autumn is on or around September 23. This change in season from summer to autumn is caused by the Earth's motion around the Sun, along with the tilt of the Earth's axis.
- Autumn is also known as *fall* because it is a time of falling leaves.
- The green pigment in leaves, *chlorophyll,* breaks down in fall. Then the leaves' bright colors—such as red, yellow, and orange—are revealed.
- The first full moon in autumn is known as the *harvest moon.*
- When monarch butterflies migrate in autumn, they travel 10 to 15 miles per hour, covering at least 80 miles a day.
- During autumn, some insects burrow underground, migrate from above to below water, or enter a different life stage.
- In autumn, squirrels prepare for winter by storing acorns in the ground or under fallen leaves. A good memory and sense of smell help them find their acorns in the winter.

Fall Flip Book

Youngsters will flip over this creative autumn project! Brainstorm with students things they hear, see, and do during fall as you record their ideas on the chalkboard. Then have each student fold a 12" x 18" sheet of white construction paper in half lengthwise. Help each youngster cut the top portion of his paper to the fold in four equal sections (see illustration). Next instruct him to write each letter of the word *fall* on a separate section and decorate it as desired. Have him lift the first section, then draw and label something that is related to fall and begins with *f.* Encourage youngsters to refer to the brainstormed list as they work. Have each student continue with the remaining sections of his flip book in a like manner. Then display youngsters' completed work on a brightly colored bulletin board titled "Books To Flip Over."

A Harvest Of Autumn Literature

Nuts To You! by Lois Ehlert (Harcourt Brace Jovanovich, Publishers; 1993)

Fall Is Here! I Love It! by Elaine W. Good (Good Books®, 1994)

The Squirrel And The Moon by Eleonore Schmid (North-South Books Inc., 1996)

Autumn: An Alphabet Acrostic by Steven Schnur (Clarion Books, 1997)

Autumn

Initial consonants: *b, f, m, s, t*

Armfuls Of Acorns

Cut.

Glue.

t	s	m	f	b

Bonus Box: On the back of this sheet, draw things that begin with *m*—such as a monkey.

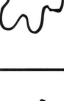

Name _____

Beyond "Be-leaf"

Color by the code.

Color Code

c — red
d — blue
l — green
p — yellow
r — orange

Bonus Box: On the back of this sheet, draw things that begin with *l*—such as a leaf.

Count On Fall

 Write.

 Cut. Glue.

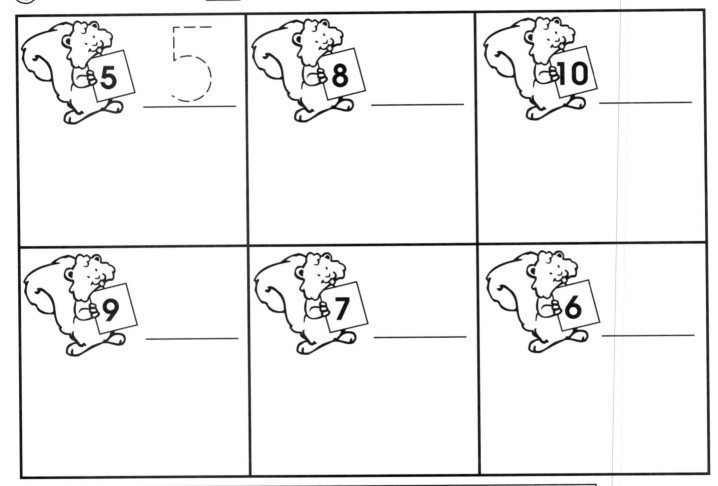

©1998 The Education Center, Inc. • *September Monthly Reproducibles* • Grade 1 • TEC956

Name _____

Autumn Opposites

Look at the pictures.
Match the opposites.

✂ Cut.

🍶 Glue.

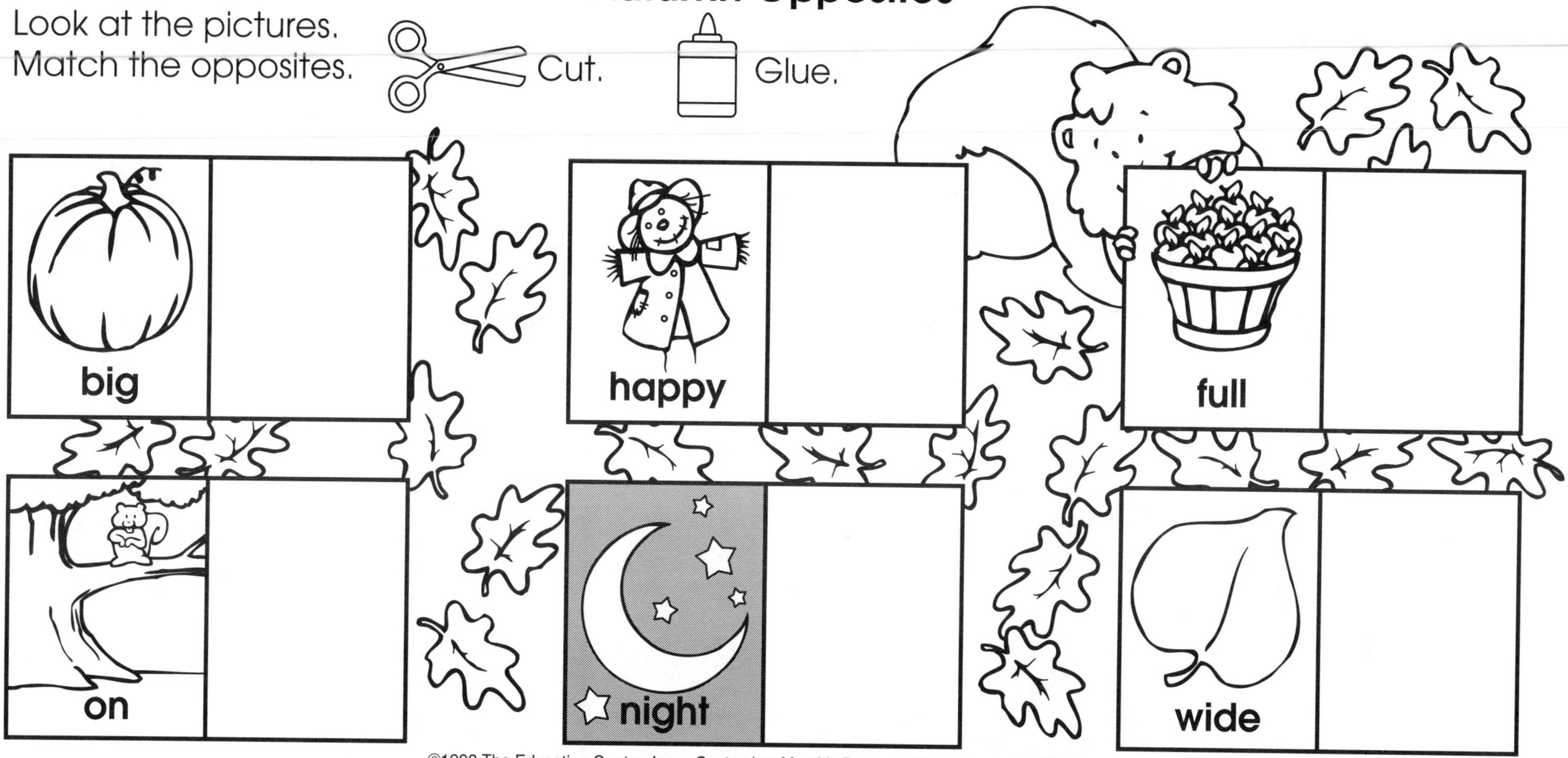

full

wide

happy

night

big

on

day

sad

off

little

empty

narrow

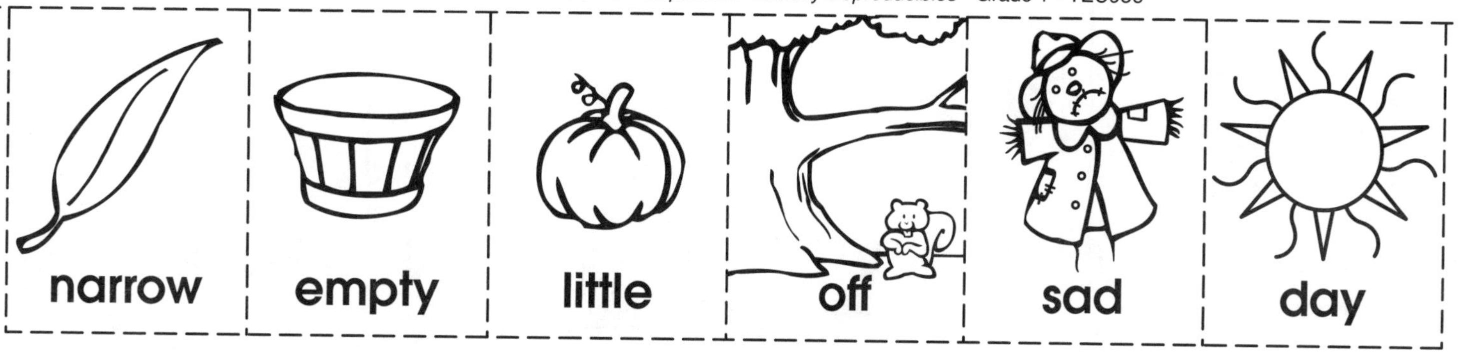

Name _____

Acorn Addition

How many acorns in all?

✏️ Write.

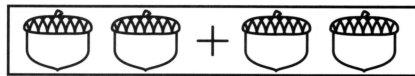

=

=

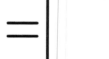 =

=

✂️ Cut out the acorns. Use them to help you add.

✏️ Write.

$2 + 3 =$		$4 + 1 =$	

$5 + 1 =$		$3 + 3 =$	

Bonus Box: On the back of this sheet, draw 2 red apples and 4 green apples. Write an addition problem to show how many in all.

Tomie dePaola

Happy birthday, Mr. dePaola! Blow out the candles on September 15 for this famous children's artist and storyteller.

Tools Of The Trade

Tomie dePaola knew at an early age that he wanted to be an artist. He still remembers how thrilled he was to receive a box of 64 crayons—a world of color at his fingertips! He used this memory to inspire his book *The Art Lesson* (The Putnam Publishing Group, 1997), a tale that young schoolchildren can easily relate to.

Share *The Art Lesson* with your students; then put their artistic talents to use to make individual word banks of art-related vocabulary. Write the desired vocabulary words on the chalkboard. Discuss each word with your students and point out its illustration in the story. Next give each child a sheet of white construction paper folded into sections for the desired amount of words. Instruct her to copy and illustrate a word from the chalkboard in each section. Allow time to complete the activity; then place students into small groups to read and discuss their word banks.

crayon   brush   pencil

paint   paper   easel

Grandparents Are Great!

Now One Foot, Now The Other (The Putnam Publishing Group, 1981) and *Nana Upstairs & Nana Downstairs* (The Putnam Publishing Group, 1998) are based on Mr. dePaola's memories of his grandparents. Since September is the month for honoring grandparents (see pages 15–18), these two tales are especially timely to share with your students. After reading the stories to your class, encourage each child to illustrate a memory he has about his grandparent or other special adult. Reinforce summary skills by having the student dictate a sentence or two about the picture for you to add as a caption. Send the projects home as gifts to delight a special grandparent on his day of honor.

My granny makes the best cookies!

Strega Nona's Magic

Your children will delight in the tale of *Strega Nona* (Simon & Schuster Books For Young Readers, 1997), a magical little lady who has a way with pasta. After hearing of her adventure in a town overrun with noodles, continue the fun with a pasta graphing activity. Provide each student with a small bag of pasta shells, elbows, and spirals. Have each child sort her pasta according to shape. Next have her arrange the pasta on her desk to make a bar graph. Encourage each student to share a statement about her graph.

Afterward, treat your little ones to a pasta-tasting party by serving a variety of pasta that has been cooked, drained, and mixed with one of the following: canned cheddar cheese soup, prepared spaghetti sauce, butter and Parmesan cheese, or condensed cream of chicken soup. (Serve warm.) What a tasty way to end a tale!

Name_____

High In The Sky

Find the pictures that rhyme.

Cut.  Glue.

tree

goat

star

log

hat

rake

©1998 The Education Center, Inc. • *September Monthly Reproducibles* • Grade 1 • TEC956

snake   cat   bee   boat   car   frog

32   **Note To The Teacher:** Use with *The Cloud Book* by Tomie dePaola (Holiday House, Inc.; 1984).

Name_____

Tomie dePaola
Color words

Crazy Colors

 Read.
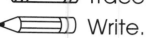 Color.
 Trace.
 Write.

red

_____

_____

_____

_____

_____

Bonus Box: On the back of this sheet, draw a funny line using your favorite color.

©1998 The Education Center, Inc. • *September Monthly Reproducibles* • Grade 1 • TEC956

Note To The Teacher: Use with *The Art Lesson* by Tomie dePaola (The Putnam Publishing Group, 1997).

Name_____

Tomie dePaola
Sequencing

Strega Nona's Story

Read.
Cut out the pictures.
Glue them in order on another piece of paper.

Strega Nona says, "You must sweep the house."

Big Anthony has to eat all the pasta.

Strega Nona tells Big Anthony he must not touch the pot!

Big Anthony sings to the pot.

Big Anthony hears the magic words.

Strega Nona goes to see her friend.

©1998 The Education Center, Inc. • *September Monthly Reproducibles* • Grade 1 • TEC956 • Key p. 64

Note To The Teacher: Share *Strega Nona* by Tomie dePaola (Simon & Schuster Books For Young Readers, 1997) with your students. Provide a 4" x 18" sheet of construction paper for each child, along with a copy of this page. Have each child glue the pieces on the strip from top to bottom.

34

National Student Day™

National Student Day™, celebrated every year on the third Thursday in September, is a time to recognize all students for their hard work and positive attitudes. Use the activities in this unit to honor and celebrate your newest constellation of shining stars!

Keeping Students In Shape

Sharpen your little stars' listening skills with this exercise in following directions. Provide each child with a copy of page 36, a pencil, and crayons. Read the following directions aloud. Pause after each item until each child completes the direction. Then challenge each child to color all the shapes on the page using the color code. No doubt your youngsters' listening skills will be in shape after this workout!

Directions:
1. Draw a circle between the triangle and the square.
2. Draw a rectangle below the circle.
3. Draw a square above rectangle C.
4. Draw a square below the triangle.
5. Draw a triangle below rectangle C.
6. Draw a circle above square B.
7. Draw a rectangle above triangle A.

Star Students

This fun project will add a delightful twinkle to your classroom while featuring all of your shining stars. Make several star-shaped tracers (approximately 12" wide). Instruct each child to trace and cut a star shape from a 12" x 18" sheet of yellow construction paper. Next help each child trace his hands onto colored construction paper and cut out the resulting shapes. Then help each student trace his feet onto colorful construction paper and cut out the resulting shapes. Direct each child in gluing his hand and foot cutouts to the star points as shown. Finally, encourage him to color a face on his silly star character and label it with his name. Display each child's twinkling twin on a bulletin board titled "[teacher's name]'s Star Students."

Awesome Awards

Every student will feel like a star wearing his Star-Student Spectacles and a Superstar Badge. Duplicate the patterns on page 37 onto tagboard for each child. To make the spectacles, have the child cut along the heavy solid lines. (If desired, use an X-acto® knife to cut the lens openings from the glasses.) Carefully cut along the broken lines labeled A and B and assemble the glasses using the matching letters. To complete the superstar badge, have each child write his name in the star; then have him write words to describe himself. (If desired, have each child dictate words as you write them on his award.) Have each child cut his award on the heavy solid outline. Then attach a piece of masking tape to the badge so he can proudly wear it on his shirt.

Name _____

36

Listening Lessons

Listen and do.
Color by the code.

Color Code:
◯ = blue
▢ = red
△ = yellow
▭ = green

A

B

C

Bonus Box: Draw another blue shape. Use the code.

Note To The Teacher: Use with "Keeping Students In Shape" on page 35.

Star-Student Spectacles

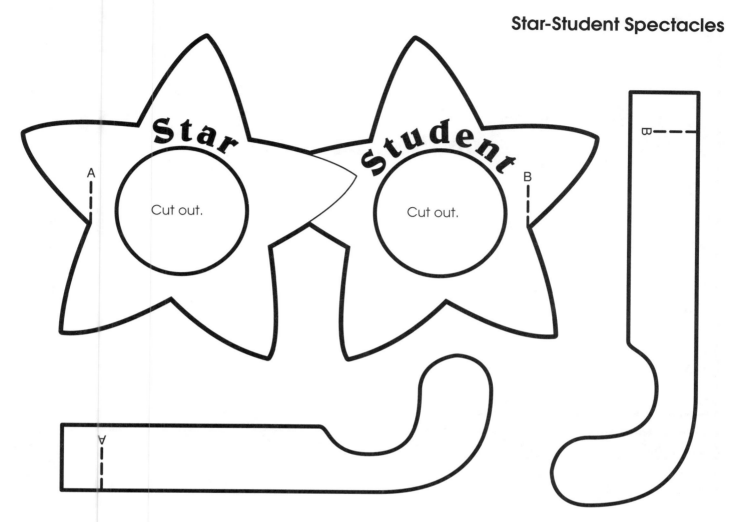

©1998 The Education Center, Inc. • *September Monthly Reproducibles* • Grade 1 • TEC956

Superstar Badge

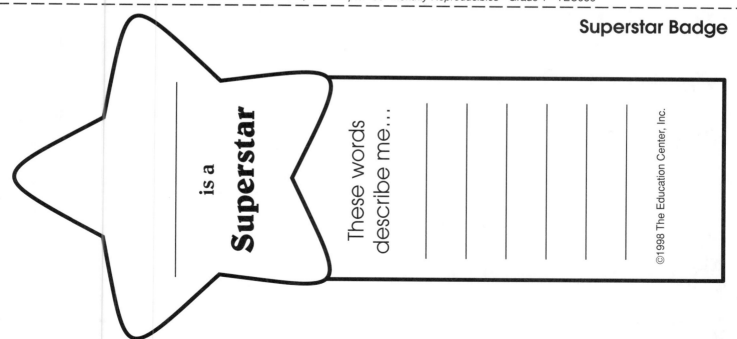

Three cheers for

_____!

You're a
superstar because

_____

_____

_____

Teacher _____ Date _____

_____

is a star-spangled student
because

_____

_____

_____

Teacher _____

Date _____

WINGED WONDERS

With this owlish collection of activities,
students will have a hootin' good time!

An owl has three
sets of eyelids.

An owl can turn its
head more than half-
way around its body.

Owls cannot move
their eyeballs.

An owl can hear
a mouse about
65 feet away.

Home, Sweet Home

Youngsters will feel right at home with this owlish booklet project! First tell students about some of the many places in which owls live. Some owls live in nests in hollows of trees. Cacti are homes to elf owls. And barn owls make their homes in barn rafters. Give each youngster a copy of page 42 and read each sentence with students. Then have each student color and cut out his booklet pieces. Direct him to stack his pages atop the owl and staple them near the top of the cover page. Have each youngster complete his booklet by gluing the beak to his owl as shown. After he reads his booklet, encourage each student to "visit" the world of owls by sharing his project with family members.

Orderly Owls

Count on these fine-feathered friends to re-inforce sequencing skills! Give each student a copy of page 44. Identify, with youngsters, each numeral shown; then ask them what they notice about these numerals. After verify-ing that the numerals are out of order, tell stu-dents that it is their job to arrange the owls in the correct numerical order. Have each stu-dent cut out his squares; sequence them nu-merically; then glue them in order on a long strip of construction paper, on sentence strips, or on a length of adding-machine tape. Next ask each student to color his owls, being careful to leave the numerals visible. For added learning fun, challenge students to identify the pattern made by the owls *(eye-glasses, hat, hat, bow)* and ask them to pre-dict what the 16th owl would wear.

"Whooo" Said?

This predictable animal story will be the talk of the class! Encourage children to chime in with you as you read aloud Pat Hutchins' *Good-Night, Owl!* (Aladdin Paperbacks, 1990). In this cumulative tale, Owl wants some peace and quiet so that he can sleep. Yet all of the forest sounds—from the buzzing bees to the cooing doves—prevent him from getting the rest he so desperately wants. Re-read the story, asking students to pay particular attention to the sound each animal makes. Then give each young-ster a copy of page 41, crayons, scis-sors, and glue. Have each student color and cut out the animals at the bottom of his page. Next read each speech bubble with students, and have each youngster glue the corresponding animal beside its sound. Challenge students to complete the Bonus Box activity, too. You can be sure that this activity will be a "re-sound-ing" success!

Name _____

40

Branch Out With The ABCs!

Write the ABCs.

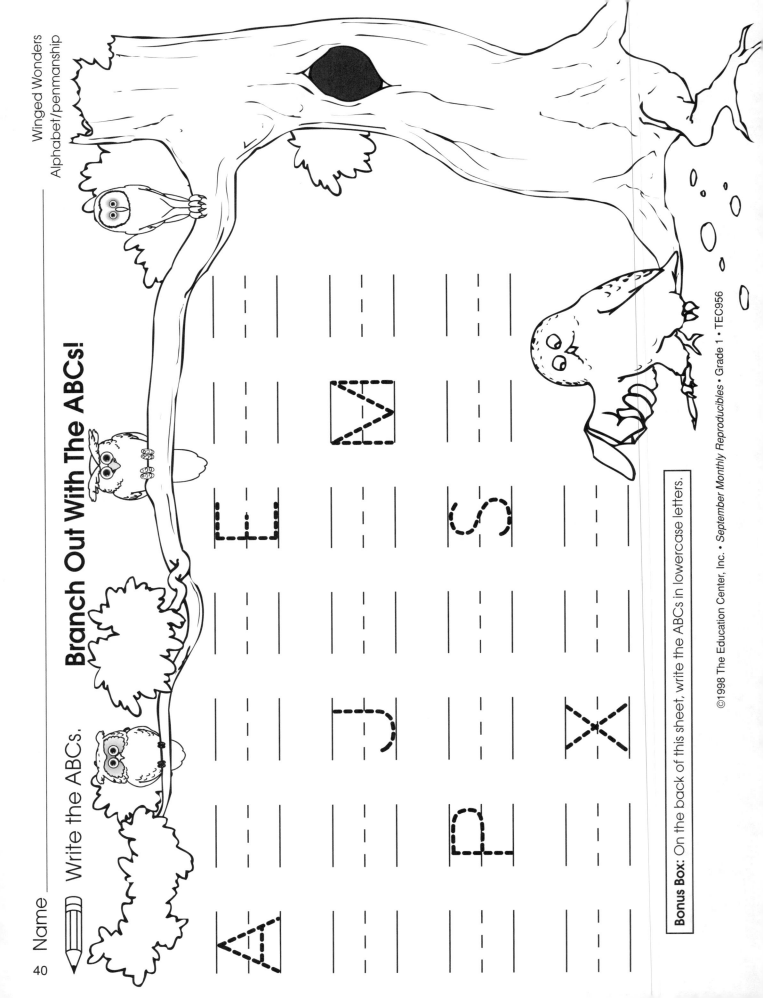

Bonus Box: On the back of this sheet, write the ABCs in lowercase letters.

Name _____

"Whooo" Said?

Color.

Cut.

Glue.

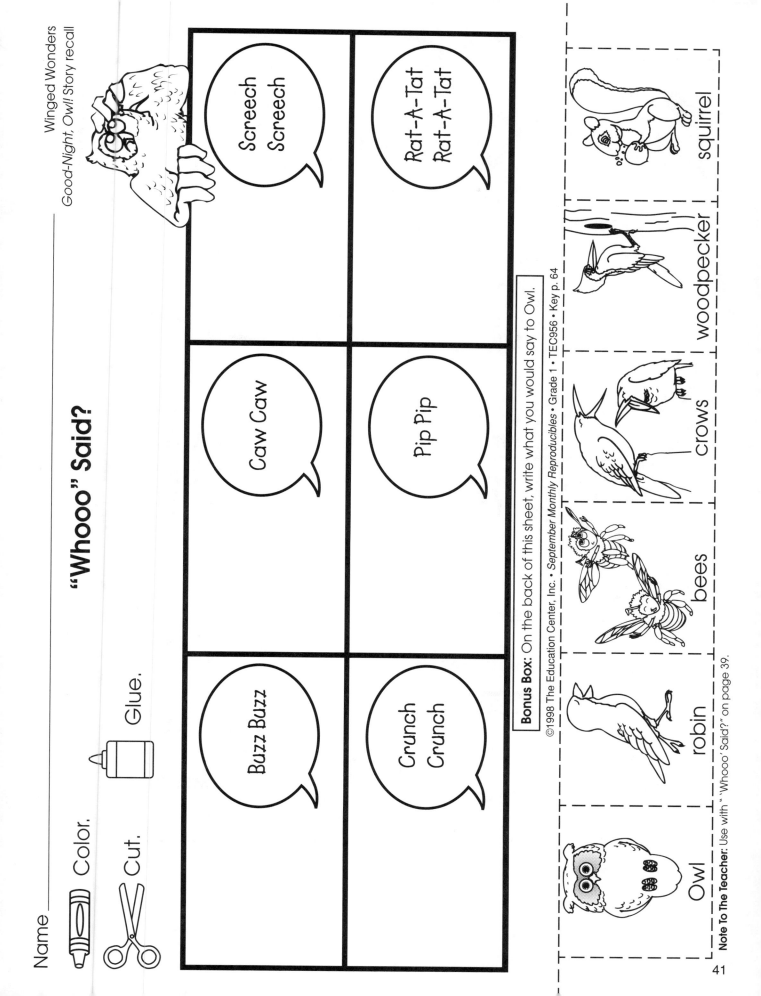

Screech Screech

Rat-A-Tat Rat-A-Tat

Caw Caw

Pip Pip

Buzz Buzz

Crunch Crunch

squirrel

woodpecker

crows

bees

robin

Owl

Bonus Box: On the back of this sheet, write what you would say to Owl.

©1998 The Education Center, Inc. • *September Monthly Reproducibles* • Grade 1 • TEC956 • Key p. 64

Note To The Teacher: Use with "Whooo' Said?" on page 39.

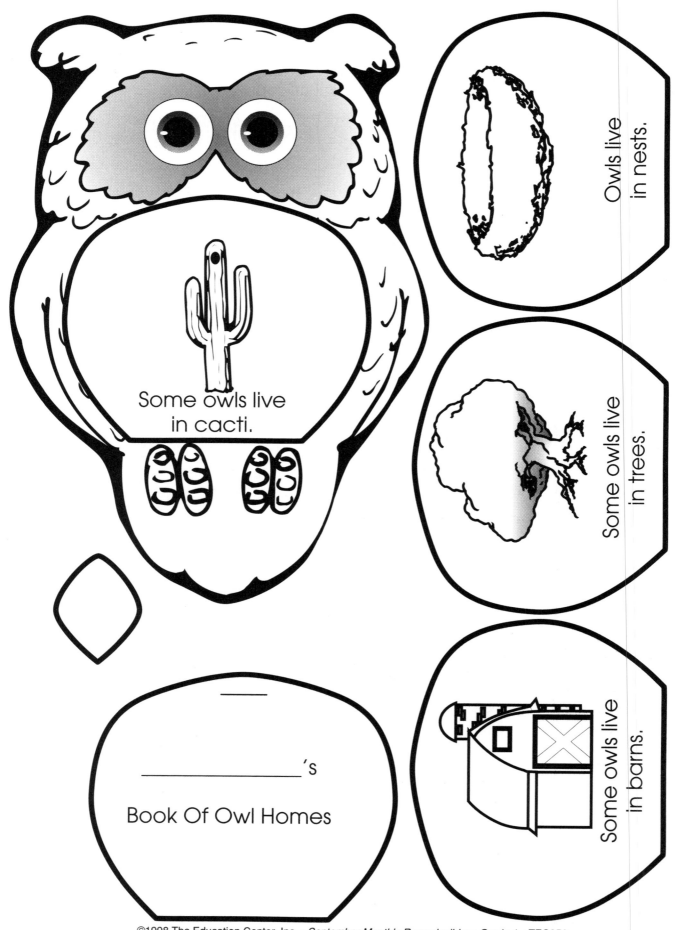

Some owls live
in cacti.

Owls live
in nests.

Some owls live
in trees.

Some owls live
in barns.

_____'s

Book Of Owl Homes

Name _____

Letter Mix-Up

Read the clues.
Write each letter in the correct car.

A is in the middle.

T is first.

R is between **T** and **A**.

I is not last.

N is one of the letters.

What did you spell? _____

Bonus Box: Make an X above the letter that is before **I** and after **R.**

Name _____

Orderly Owls

✂ Cut.

🧴 Glue in order.

5	13	6	11	8
9	3	14	10	12
1	7	2	15	4

Note To The Teacher: Use with "Orderly Owls" on page 39.

CITIZENSHIP DAY

Citizenship Day, observed on September 17, is a proud and patriotic combination of two former holidays: Constitution Day and I Am An American Day. Many immigrants take their oath of American allegiance on this day. Your students can observe the holiday by discussing what it means to be true to the red, white, and blue.

PATRIOTIC PARADE

As students readily recognize the flag, the Statue of Liberty, and other patriotic symbols of our country, provide them with the opportunity to show what they know in a poster parade. Provide each student with a sheet of white construction paper and crayons or markers. Instruct him to illustrate a patriotic symbol of our country. When the posters are completed, lead the students in a march through other classrooms to show their patriotic prowess. Afterward have students toast the USA with a special punch made by adding red- and blue-tinted ice cubes to lemon-lime soda.

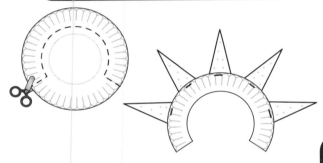

LADY LIBERTY

One of the most sensational symbols of our country is the Statue of Liberty, a sign of welcome and promise of freedom to those who enter the United States. Familiarize your students with this striking sculpture by having them dress the part. Provide each student with a paper plate and instruct him to cut from the center as shown. Next provide a triangle tracer, and have him trace and cut out five white construction-paper triangles. Help him apply a thin coat of glue to his triangles and add a sprinkle of glitter to each shape. After the glue dries, assist him in stapling the points to the paper plate as shown. Encourage each child to don his crown at home as he explains the patriotic symbolism of Lady Liberty.

OUR STARS AND STRIPES

The American flag is a symbol of the land and people of the United States. When we pledge to the flag, we give our promise to be loyal to our country. Help your students appreciate the history of our flag by sharing these special facts:

- The 50 stars represent our 50 states.
- The 13 stripes represent the 13 original colonies.
- The red stripes stand for courage.
- The white stripes stand for liberty.
- The field of blue stands for loyalty.
- Our flag has nicknames. It is sometimes called "Old Glory" or "The Stars And Stripes."

Bring the lesson to a tasty conclusion by having each student make a flag treat from graham crackers, frosting, and red string licorice. Have each student frost her cracker with white and blue frosting to resemble a flag. Next have her add the red licorice for stripes. For a final touch, instruct her to use a toothpick to dab white frosting "stars" to her edible creation.

Name _____

Symbol Sort

Cut out the pictures.
Glue the U.S. symbols.
Cut out the badge.
Wear.

Note To The Teacher: Discuss U.S. symbols with your students; then distribute a copy of this page to each child. After the badges are complete, provide loops of masking tape for attaching the badges to students' shirts.

Name _____

Winning Words

Cut.

Glue.

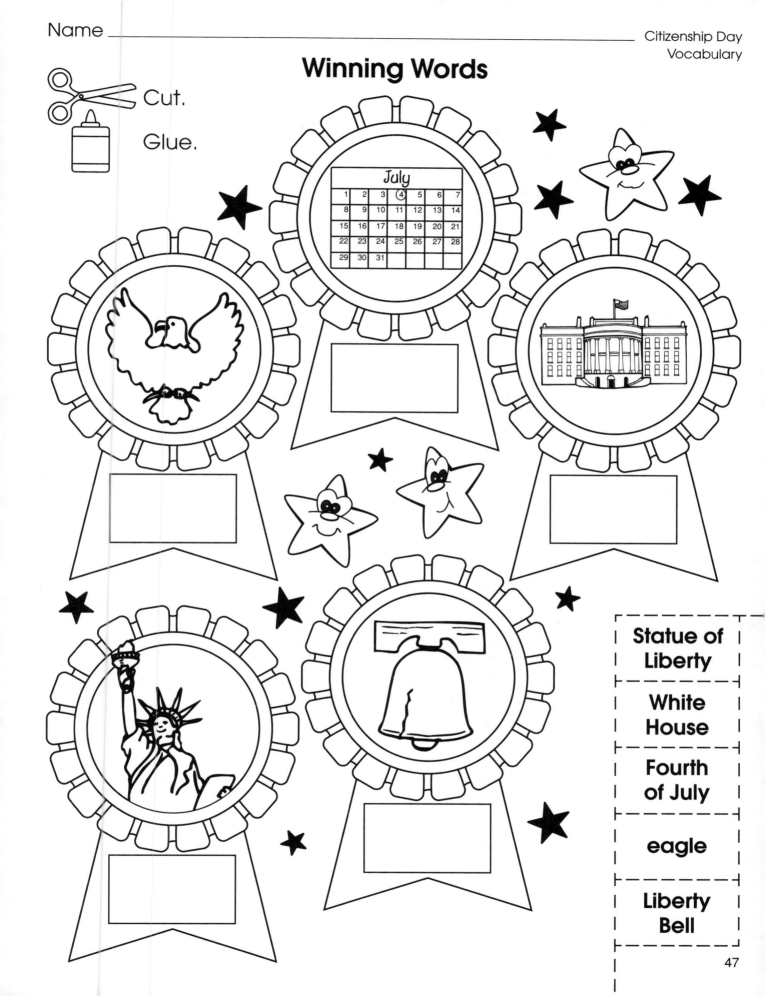

| Statue of Liberty |
| White House |
| Fourth of July |
| eagle |
| Liberty Bell |

Name _____

See The USA

Read.
Color.

I live in the _____ .

I see the brown _____ .

I see the yellow _____ .

I see the green _____ .

I see the red, white, and blue _____ .

I live in the USA!

Draw.

Note To The Teacher: Have each child draw a likeness of himself in the last box.

Ice Cream Month

Get The Scoop!

September is a time to recognize a dessert that's irresistible to many—ice cream. "Dip" into this tasty topic by sharing these flavorful facts with students.

- More ice cream is produced and eaten in the United States than in any other country.
- Vanilla is the most popular ice-cream flavor in the United States.
- No one is certain when ice cream was first made.
- Ice-cream *sundays* were sold only on Sundays in the 1890s. When people began eating this dessert on other days, the spelling was changed to *sundaes*.
- One of the first ice-cream sandwiches was made with oatmeal cookies and vanilla ice cream. It was called the *It's It Bar*.

Order, Please!

Give students a taste of ordinal numbers with this luscious lineup! Distribute a copy of page 53 to each student and review with youngsters the ordinal numbers and words featured. Then have each student cut apart his ice-cream desserts and glue them in order on a paper strip that is approximately 6" x 24". Top off this sweet activity by having students follow directions such as the ones shown. Seconds, anyone?

Add a cherry to the eighth dessert.

Add a scoop of ice cream to the fifth dessert.

Draw nuts on the second dessert.

Add sprinkles to the tenth dessert.

Draw a straw in the third dessert.

Flavors From *A* To *Z*

Invent tempting ice-cream flavors, letter by letter, with this mouthwatering class-book project! Brainstorm ice-cream flavors with students and record them on the chalkboard. Then assign each letter of the alphabet to a student. (Depending on your class size, some students may need to work with more than one letter.) Explain to youngsters that they will use their imaginations to develop new flavors. Encourage them to refer to the brainstormed list for ideas and to be creative— maybe inventing nifty new flavors such as Wild Berry Bonanza or more zany flavors such as Spinach Supreme or Peppy Pizza. On a large sheet of paper, have each student write the following sentence frame: [letter], my name is [name] and I like [flavor] ice cream. Have him complete the sentence with his letter and a name and flavor that begin with the letter. Direct each student to add an illustration; then bind students' completed work in alphabetical order between construction-paper covers. Add the title "Flavors From *A* To *Z*" and decorate the cover as desired. For an extra-special treat, serve ice-cream desserts after reading aloud this tantalizing book. Mmmm…delicious!

Name _____

Cool Cones

Write each matching lowercase letter.

F

R

T

D

C

M

H

S

Bonus Box: On the back of this sheet, write the alphabet in lowercase letters.

©1998 The Education Center, Inc. • *September Monthly Reproducibles* • Grade 1 • TEC956

Name

Tasty Treats

Trace.

Cut.

Glue

Bonus Box: On the back of this sheet, draw things that begin with *n*—such as a nut.

Name _____

Delicious Desserts

Count.

Cut.

Glue.

1 one	**2** two	**3** three	**4** four
5 five	**6** six	**7** seven	**8** eight
9 nine	**10** ten		

Ice Cream month
Ordinal numbers

Order, Please!

Follow your teacher's directions.

5th fifth	**9th** ninth
3rd third	**7th** seventh
8th eighth	**2nd** second
1st first	**4th** fourth
6th sixth	**10th** tenth

©1998 The Education Center, Inc. • *September Monthly Reproducibles* • Grade 1 • TEC956

Note To The Teacher: Use with "Order, Please!" on page 49.

Name _____

Triple-Scoop Delight

Color.

Complete the graph.

green																
brown																
pink																

   1   2   3   4   5   6   7   8   9   10   11   12   13   14   15   16

Answer the questions.

1. How many scoops are green *or* pink? _____

2. How many *more* scoops are brown than

   green? _____

Bonus Box: On the back of this sheet, write two sentences about your graph.

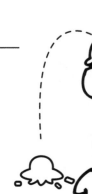

©1998 The Education Center, Inc. • *September Monthly Reproducibles* • Grade 1 • TEC956

NATIONAL
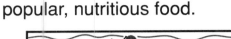
CHICKEN MONTH

What is the most celebrated bird of the month? The chicken! September, known as National Chicken Month, is an "egg-cellent" time to spotlight this popular, nutritious food.

Little Chicks

These "hand-some" creations are as much fun to make as they are to look at. Give each child a 12" x 18" sheet of white construction paper. Prepare several containers, each containing a different color of tempera paint and a brush. Have each child take a turn at painting the palm of her hand with a desired color. Then have her press her hand onto her paper to make a print. Encourage her to make several handprints on her paper before setting it aside to dry. After the paint is dry, have her use markers to add a beak on the thumb portion of each print and chicken feet to the bottom as shown. Encourage your students to color barnyard scenes to surround these fancy fowl.

What's your favorite way to eat chicken?			
fried	grilled	nuggets	soup

Charting Chickens

Improve your students' graphing skills with this collection of chicken-charting options. Create a large, reusable graph on a classroom bulletin board or wall. Use one of the following questions to collect data for each graphing experience. Then have students record their answers on the graph by taping chicken-shaped cutouts to it.
Questions:
- What is your favorite way to eat chicken? *(fried, grilled, nuggets, soup)*
- What is your favorite way to eat eggs? *(fried, scrambled, hard-boiled, omelette)*
- How often does your family eat chicken? *(never, sometimes, often)*
- Do you like to eat chicken? *(yes, no)*

An "Egg-citing" Alphabet

"Chick" out this fun activity that's just right for reinforcing letter-recognition skills. Duplicate page 57 and a copy of the lowercase letter squares on this page for each child. Have each child cut apart his letter squares along the broken lines. Then challenge him to match each lowercase letter to an egg with the appropriate uppercase letter. Provide a small envelope for each child to use for storing his squares between uses.

For added interest, try this partner variation. Have each child store his letter squares and his four chicken squares in his envelope; then pair students. Ask one child from each pair to pull a square from his envelope and place it on the matching letter on page 57. If he draws a chicken, he loses his turn. Have the partners take turns drawing and placing letter squares. The first child to cover all of his letters is the winner.

Lowercase Letter Squares

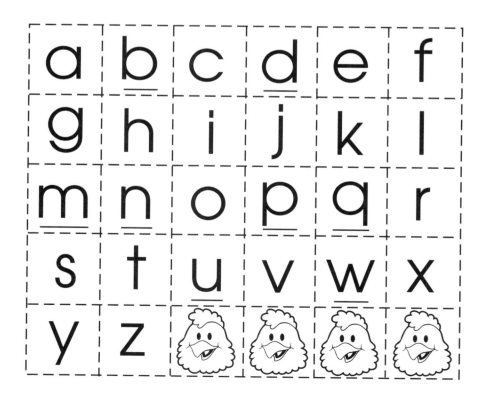

An "Egg-citing" Alphabet

Listen and do.

A B C D E F G H I J K L M N O P Q R S T U V W X Y Z

Note To The Teacher: Use with "An 'Egg-citing' Alphabet" on page 56.

Name _____

58

Egg Hunt

Listen and do.

Bonus Box: How many eggs did the hen find? Label each egg with a number as you count.

©1998 The Education Center, Inc. • *September Monthly Reproducibles* • Grade 1 • TEC956

Note To The Teacher: Read the following directions aloud: (1) Draw one egg to the left of the barn. (2) Draw three eggs to the right of the tree. (3) Draw two eggs on the haystack. (4) Draw four eggs behind the hen. (5) Draw one egg in the barn.

NATIONAL HONEY MONTH

Why all the buzz about honey? Because September is officially National Honey Month! This distinguished celebration is held not only to recognize the wholesome goodness of honey, but also to honor its producer—the honeybee. Celebrate this honey of a holiday with the following activities and reproducibles.

What's The Source?

Give your students a quick lesson on food sources with the help of *A Cow, A Bee, A Cookie, And Me* by Meredith Hooper (Kingfisher, 1997). Before sharing the story, purchase the ingredients listed on the last page of the book. Display each of the ingredients on a table in your classroom. (Leave the items in their containers and don't separate the egg until after you share the story.) Show your students one ingredient at a time, and ask each child to share where he thinks the item first came from. (You may need to prompt their thinking to a source besides the grocery store.) Then read the story aloud to your students. If desired, stop and display each ingredient after you read about it in the text. Your students will be amazed at some of the ingredients' origins. Follow up the story by helping your students make the book's honey cookies using the recipe at the end of the book. Your students will love this literature *and* the tasty treat!

liquid honey

sweet sticky gooey

dry sweet crunchy

honey graham crackers

Taste, Tell, And Tally

Honey is an ingredient in a variety of favorite foods. Try this graphing activity with your students to introduce them to an assortment of products that include honey. Purchase several different food items that are flavored with honey. For each product, make a large bee cutout from yellow poster board. (Do not draw stripes on the bee cutouts). Write a different honey-flavored item on each of the bees; then mount them at the bottom of a chalkboard or a bulletin board covered in paper. Serve each child a sampling of one honey-flavored food. Ask your students to describe the food; then write their descriptive words above the appropriate bee cutout. Repeat the process for the remaining foods. After tasting all of the honey-flavored products, ask each child to select a favorite by drawing a black stripe on the bee labeled with her choice. Count the stripes to sum up your students' favorite honey food.

Making A Beeline

Count.
Write.
Draw a line to match.

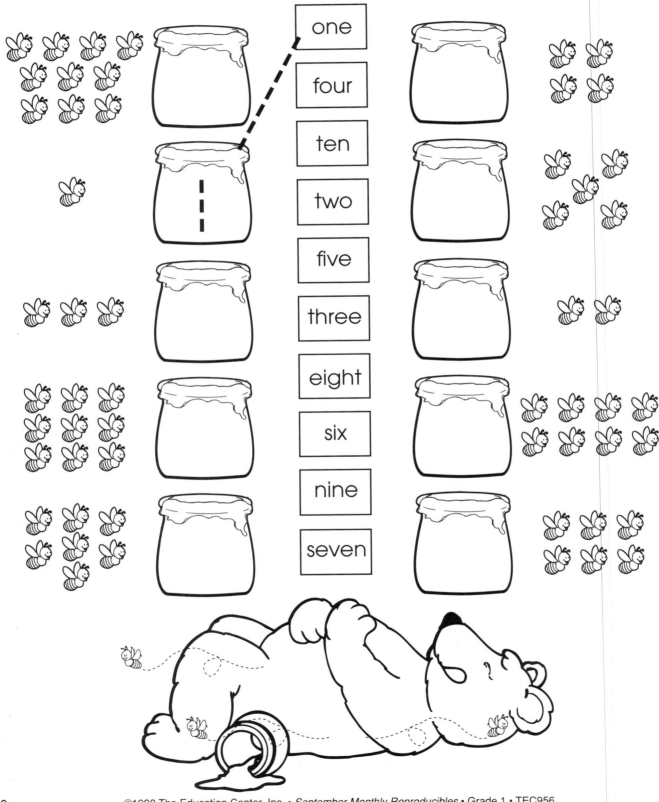

one
four
ten
two
five
three
eight
six
nine
seven

Name _____

A Sweet Start

Name the pictures.
Write each beginning sound.

_____ ‑ ‑ ‑ ‑ _____	_____ ‑ ‑ ‑ ‑ _____	_____ ‑ ‑ ‑ ‑ _____

_____ ‑ ‑ ‑ ‑ _____	_____ ‑ ‑ ‑ ‑ _____	_____ ‑ ‑ ‑ ‑ _____
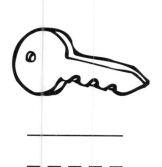		
_____ ‑ ‑ ‑ ‑ _____	_____ ‑ ‑ ‑ ‑ _____	_____ ‑ ‑ ‑ ‑ _____

Bonus Box: On the back
of this sheet, draw some
things that begin with *p.*

Name _____

Cut out the bees.
Use them to help you add.
Write.

$\begin{array}{r} 2 \\ + 3 \\ \hline \end{array}$

$\begin{array}{r} 3 \\ + 3 \\ \hline \end{array}$

$\begin{array}{r} 0 \\ + 6 \\ \hline \end{array}$

$\begin{array}{r} 2 \\ + 5 \\ \hline \end{array}$

$\begin{array}{r} 5 \\ + 1 \\ \hline \end{array}$

$\begin{array}{r} 3 \\ + 4 \\ \hline \end{array}$

$\begin{array}{r} 4 \\ + 2 \\ \hline \end{array}$

$\begin{array}{r} 7 \\ + 0 \\ \hline \end{array}$

$\begin{array}{r} 1 \\ + 4 \\ \hline \end{array}$

$\begin{array}{r} 2 \\ + 2 \\ \hline \end{array}$

©1998 The Education Center, Inc. • *September Monthly Reproducibles* • Grade 1 • TEC956

Honey-Pot Patterns

Cut.
Glue to finish each pattern.

Glue to make your own pattern.

Answer Keys

Page 34

Strega Nona says, "You must sweep the house."

Strega Nona tells Big Anthony he must not touch the pot!

Big Anthony hears the magic words.

Strega Nona goes to see her friend.

Big Anthony sings to the pot.

Big Anthony has to eat all the pasta.

Page 41

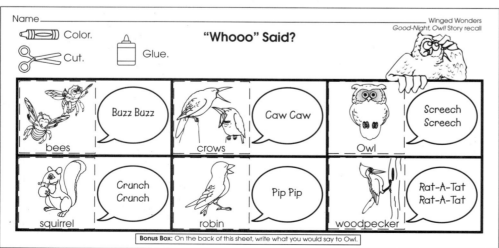

Name_____

Winged Wonders
Good-Night, Owl! Story recall

Color.   Cut.   Glue.

"Whooo" Said?

bees — Buzz Buzz	crows — Caw Caw	Owl — Screech Screech
squirrel — Crunch Crunch	robin — Pip Pip	woodpecker — Rat-A-Tat Rat-A-Tat

Bonus Box: On the back of this sheet, write what you would say to Owl.

64